I0429827

"ALIEN COMMUN- ICATION WORKBOOK"

A BRIEF ILLUSTRATED GUIDE FOR COMMUNICATING WITH EXTRA- TERRESTRIALS

Nathan Coppedge

NATHAN COPPEDGE

INTRODUCTION:

By the end of this guide you should have a better idea of what it means to communicate with an extra-terrestrial.

Although there are some intrinsic fears, the guide offers the same approach which is likely to be encountered on the path to genuine communication, namely a work-intensive technique, following the mantra of:

"Just add it to the pile"

This technique might combine with other techniques to benefit long-term knowledge.

For example, what sort of word-play do extra-terrestrials use?

What sorts of questions do they, or might they ask?

Who are they really interested in?

And finally, the open-ended question, of what do we really think? And how is it appropriate to react?

All of these questions are raised in this short booklet, with an eye towards long-term solutions to the communications problem (or, perhaps problems to it's solution, in alien-speak).

THE WORKBOOK

SOMEONE MAY GO TO
PLUTO AND TALK TO DUST
GRAINS

BUT THEY MAY AS WELL
TALK TO YOU!

IF THERE ARE ALIENS ON
PLUTO, THEY WOULD BE
FRIENDS WITH THEM, TOO!

IT'S BUSINESS-AS-USUAL,
AND FINALLY THEY PICK UP
A CONVERSATION, IN YOUR
OWN WELL-DEFINED NA-
TIVE LANGUAGE

WHAT IF YOUR ALIEN
FRIEND SAYS:

1. PLEASED TO MEET YOU!

<u>AND</u>

2. THEY WOULD LIKE TO
HAVE YOUR <u>ANIMAL</u> OVER
FOR LUNCH?

AND IT TURNS OUT WHAT
THEY MEAN IS:

1. THEY WANT TO HAVE
   LUNCH,

<u>AND</u>

2. THEY WANT THE PLEAS-
URE OF YOUR COMPANION?

WHAT IF THEY MEAN THAT
THEY WANT TO EAT YOU
AND YOUR COMPANION,
TOO?

WHAT IF THEY MEAN THAT
THEY WANT LUNCH AND
WANT TO MOLEST YOUR
DOG?

WHAT IF THEY ARE NAIVELY
INTERESTED IN YOU YOUR-
SELF?

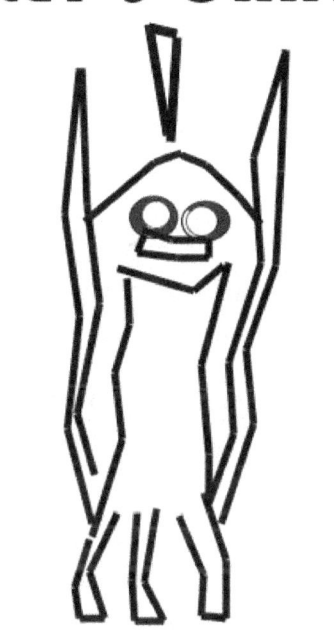

IN SOME WAYS, A PLEASANT
LUNCH IS THE LEAST
LIKELY THING!

WHAT ARE YOU SUPPOSED
TO THINK?

IS IT A METAPHYSICAL
QUESTION?

AT WHAT POINT DOES YOUR
FAX COLLAPSE?

I WANT YOU TO ANSWER SINCERELY ON THE FOL-LOWING PAGES:

_____

_____

_____

_____

_____

_____

_____

_____

_____

_____

_____

_____

_____

_____

_____

_____

_____

_____

_____

_____

_____

_____

_____

_____

_____

_____

_____

_____

_____

_____

NATHAN COPPEDGE

_____

_____

_____

_____

_____

_____

_____

_____

_____

_____

_____

_____

_____

_____

_____

_____

_____

_____

_____

_____

_____

_____

_____

_____

_____

_____

_____

_____

_____

_____

_____

_____

_____

_____

_____

NATHAN COPPEDGE

_____

_____

_____

_____

_____

_____

_____

_____

_____

_____

_____

_____

_____

_____

_____

_____

_____

_____

_____

_____

_____

_____

_____

_____

_____

_____

_____

_____

_____

_____

_____

_____

_____

_____

_____

_____

_____

_____

_____

_____

_____

_____

_____

_____

_____

_____

_____

_____

_____

_____

_____

_____

_____

_____

_____

_____

_____

_____

_____

_____

_____

_____

_____

_____

_____

_____

_____

_____

_____

_____

_____

_____

_____

_____

_____

_____

_____

_____

_____

_____

_____

_____

_____

_____

_____

_____

_____

_____

_____

ALIEN COMMUNICATION WORKBOOK

_____

_____

_____

_____

_____

_____

_____

_____

_____

_____

_____

_____

_____

_____

_____

_____

_____

_____

_____

_____

_____

NATHAN COPPEDGE

———————————————————————
———————————————————————
———————————————————————
———————————————————————
———————————————————————
———————————————————————
———————————————————————
———————————————————————
———————————————————————
———————————————————————
———————————————————————
———————————————————————
———————————————————————
———————————————————————
———————————————————————
———————————————————————
———————————————————————
———————————————————————
———————————————————————

ALIEN COMMUNICATION WORKBOOK

_____

_____

_____

_____

_____

_____

_____

_____

_____

_____

_____

_____

_____

_____

_____

_____

_____

_____

_____

_____

_____

_____
_____
_____
_____
_____
_____
_____
_____
_____
_____
_____
_____
_____
_____
_____
_____
_____
_____
_____
_____
_____
_____

COMMUNICATING WITH EX-TRA-TERRESTRIALS

An Outline of Assumptions

1. They may be human-like, in which case there is potential for common ground.
2. If they are very different, there is potential to treat them like endangered species.
3. If they are much more advanced, there is potential to learn from them.
4. The ultimate disaster is a kind of very complicated coincidence.
5. Actual dangers depend on actual potential dangers, such as weapons, stars, or abilities to change attitudes.
6. Similarly, actual benefits of correspondence depend on actual abilities to correspond.
7. Compatibility between one language or communication pattern and another must be interpreted in the sense of both languages or communication patterns, although it is NOT certain that anything will be known about the other.
8. Attempts should be made to preserve advantages and not make hasty guesses about the ultimate outcome of correspondence.
9. Ultimately, it may be important to find alliances with human-like entities even at great expense, in case there are technological outliers amongst the non-human species. This may prove difficult, but there is apparently a

lot of time in which to accomplish it.

10. One should not underestimate the ability of the universe to minimize economies which seem locally fruitful. Not only is the difference between civilizations large even on our own planet, but outside of our solar system resources may differ significantly. There is a great difference between an isolated planet and a group of planets that have already successfully coordinated or become an empire of one original planet.

11. Fortunately, yet again, the timescale renders not only incredible potentials for profit, but considerable leeway in acquiring resources.

12. However, the amount of cleverness required to coordinate with another species, even a very similar one, has yet to be estimated.

A List of Facts of Communication:

1. An extra-terrestrial may not have a concept of love. But the central concept, if there is one, may not be opposite either.

2. Extra-terrestrials have a kind of universal mental illness, and so do humans. I say this because, assuming harsh environments, there has been a difficulty of circumstance, and a corresponding virtue of adaptation. Species are necessarily adapted to a very specific set of technicalities which are, except in the case of high thresholds of understanding, not very universal.

Possible Exceptions:

1. It is possible to gamble that humans or those like them are some of the only real species in the universe. However, given the range of environments, and the discomfort that humans often express in spite of their relative adaptivity to the local environment, it is likely there are sometimes other species which are more comfortable even within a harsher climate.

NOTES:

_____

_____

_____

_____

_____

_____

_____

_____

_____

_____

_____

_____

NATHAN COPPEDGE

_____

_____

_____

_____

_____

_____

_____

_____

_____

_____

_____

_____

_____

_____

_____

_____

_____

_____

_____

_____

ALIEN COMMUNICATION WORKBOOK

_____

_____

_____

_____

_____

_____

_____

_____

_____

_____

_____

_____

_____

_____

_____

_____

_____

_____

_____

_____

_____

_____

BIO

Nathan Coppedge is previously author of books on eclectic subjects, such as psychology, aphorisms, perpetual motion machines. He is the author of the Perpetual Motion Genius' Guide series, and is a member of the International Honor Society for Philosophy. He lives in New Haven, CT (on the planet earth, in the Milky Way Galaxy…).